mercy

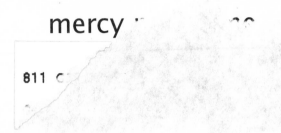

mercy mercy me

elena georgiou

Painted Leaf Press
New York City

Published in the United States by Painted Leaf Press, P.O.Box 2480, Times Square Station, New York, NY 10108-2480. Printed in Canada.

Cover design: Travis Ward
Cover photo: Marita LaMonica
Typesetting: Brian Brunius

Grateful acknowledgement is made to the editors of the following journals and anthologies in which some of these poems, or versions of these poems, have appeared:

Global City Review, Poetry Nation: The North American Anthology of Fusion Poetry, Too Darn Hot: Writing About Sex Since Kinsey, Soul: Black Power, Politics, and Pleasure, The World In Us: Lesbian and Gay Poetry of the Next Wave, Best Lesbian Erotica 1999, The Arc of Love, Feed: An Arts Magazine of Communion, The Harrington Quarterly Review, The 12-Gauge Review, The Olivetree Review, and *Poder.*

Library of Congress Cataloging-in-Publication Data

Georgiou, Elena.
    Mercy mercy me : poems / Elena Georgiou.
        p. cm.
    ISBN 1-891305-24-7
    1. New York (N.Y.)--Poetry. 2. Punk culture--Poetry.
    3. Soul music--Poetry. I. Title

    PS3557.E5 M4 2000
    811'.6--dc21

                                                    99-087728

for MAD

"You women have no major philosophers." We know.
But we remain philosophic, and say with the Saint,
"Let me enter my chamber and sing my songs of love."

—Carolyn Kizer
"The Erotic Philosophers"

Virtually every writer I know would rather be a musician...
music is the proof of the existence of God.

—Kurt Vonnegut
like shaking hands with god

CONTENTS

5   A Week In The Life Of The Ethnically Indeterminate

9   Talkin' Trash

12   Where Her Flesh Begins

14   The Space Between

16   Lessons In Honesty

20   Bang

23   Go

24   I Will Not Grow Old Wishing

29   Questions In The Mind Of A Poet As She Washes Her Floors

31   If I Could Touch Faith This Poem Would Not Exist

32   Divination

34   Sinkyone Woman Living

36   Zen And The Art Of Flower Arranging

37   Floating Poem

38   Remembrance Of Things Past

40   Approaching The Third Millennium

41   Intimate Mixture

43   Woman And Machine

45   The Science Of Kissing

46   If Picasso Had Loved Women

47   From Where I Stand

50   Sugar And Pepper

52   Hymn

54   Close Communion

56   Miracle

57   Holy Rumor

58   Sadly Mistaken

59   The State Of Our Union (Redemption Song)

61   A Sexual Revolution: From Punk Rock To Soul

66   The Motown Angel

ACKNOWLEDGEMENTS

For their generous support, I would like to thank The Astraea Foundation and The New York Foundation for the Arts.

For their teachings, I would like to thank Judith Baumel, Louise DeSalvo, Melinda Goodman, Molly Peacock, and the late Bill Mathews.

For their faith and love, I would like to thank Steve Benson, Regie Cabico, Rory Devine, Marie-Alice Devieux, Gayle DeWindt, Alex Echevarria, Melanie Hope, Michael Lassell, Mary Lefkarites, Carol Mangis, Juliet Margetts, Arnela Ten Meer, Eileen Myles, Gerry Gomez Pearlberg, Jan Poppendieck, Lisa Ross, Lauren Sanders, Dorothea Smartt, Kyra Sinkowsky, and Aaron Zimmerman.

And an almighty and limitless thank you to Debora Lidov.

Many others have also blessed me with their support: you know who you are, and I thank you.

mercy mercy me

A Week In The Life Of The Ethnically Indeterminate

MONDAY
Sitting in MacDonalds on 103rd and 3rd
I notice a couple staring at me
and hear them say *Indian.*
They walk towards me.
The woman has white skin,
blond hair, blue eyes.
The man has ebony skin,
black hair, brown eyes.
Excuse me, says the woman,
we were wondering
where you were from.
Yeah, says the man,
because you look like
our people.
I look at the whiteness
and the blackness,
wondering who their people are.
We're Puerto Rican, they say
and walk away.

TUESDAY
Walking to the store
in Crown Heights I see
an African-American man
sitting behind a table
selling incense and oils.
He calls out, Sister, hey sister,
baby, and then makes a noise

like he's calling a cat.
I don't respond.
On the way back
from the store
he calls out, *Mira, mira,*
hey baby.
In any language,
English, Feline, or Spanish
I don't respond.

WEDNESDAY
I am buying lunch
at the falafel stand
on 68th and Lex
and the man serving me asks,
You from Morocco?
No, I say, Cyprus.
Where's Cyprus? he asks.
Above Egypt
to the left of Israel
and below Turkey.
Oh, he says looking blank.
How much for the falafel, I ask?
For you three dollars.
For Americans three fifty.
I go to pay and another man
stares hard into my face
and says, Are you a Jewish chick?
No, I say, just leave me alone.
I know who you are, he screams.
I know who you are.
You're just a nigger from Harlem,
passing for white
with a phony accent.

Nigger, he repeats
as I walk away.

THURSDAY
My boss calls me up.
I have a funny question
to ask you, he says.
When you fill out forms
what do you write for ethnicity?
I check *other*, I say.
Well, I have to fill out this form
and it doesn't have *other*.
We look really bad on paper.
All the positions of power are white
and all the support staff are black.
Could you be Asian?

FRIDAY
I am with my Indian immigration lawyer.
Do you mind if I ask you
a personal question? he says.
Go ahead, I say, thinking
he is going to ask me
how I've reached my mid thirties
and have never been married.
But instead he says,
I know you're a Cypriot
from London
but do you have
any Indian blood in you?
There are so many
mixed marriages these days
and you look like the offspring.

SATURDAY
I am at a conference
and a European-American woman
looks at me excitedly
as though she's just won a prize.
Oh, I know where you're from, she says,
my daughter-in-law is an Indian
with a British accent too.
I'm not Indian, I say.
She continues to not see me
as she concentrates on
hiding her anger
for not winning the trophy
in her self-imposed
guess the ethnicity competition
and then she walks away.

SUNDAY
I go to lunch at the home of a friend
whose family are Africans of the diaspora.
They don't ask me where I'm from.
Later, my friend tells me,
They've decided you're
a biracial Jamaican.

That evening,
I'm at a poetry reading
and an African-American woman
crosses the room
to ask me this question:
Are you the colonized
or the colonizer?
What do you think? I ask.
You could be both, she responds
and walks away.

Talkin' Trash

I want the phone to ring.

I want the sound of your voice
to smack my body as waves hit rock,
grinding down mountains, opening up
secrets hidden between my shoulder blades.

I want you to beg me to let you come
over to wash my hair with rosewater.
When I refuse, I want you to hang up.

I want you to call back when I'm doing my laundry
and whine until I agree to let you be with me
the next time it's washday, so you can fold it.

I want you to ask me if I miss you.
And when I say: *Yes, I think about you
night and day,* I want you to know
I'm lying.

I want you to tell me you'd buy three bridges,
cross two oceans in a thunderstorm
to make my lie of missing you reality.

I want to tell you that for a small
part of the Caribbean Sea I'd turn into
a hungry anemone that sucks you closer.

I want you to ask me if this is all I want.
I want to tell you: *No.*

I want you to be my boy, my girl.
I want to paint your toenails gold,
massage your fingers with homemade oil
named after the smell of your neck.

I want to dust my mattress with baby powder,
lie on satin, tie ivory shells around my hips
and prepare myself for your coming.

I want you to call one last time,
ask me to unlock my door,
lie on my bed and wait.

I want to hear your bag drop to the floor,
the drag of your feet move to my bed.

I want to feel the weight of your body
sink the mattress two inches lower.

I want your arms to come from behind and
hold my breasts in an open prayer.

I want to hear you call on God
and give her credit for making me.

I want to watch you plead: *Lord
have mercy,* as you slide your mouth
from my navel to the back of my knee.

I want you to make me speak in tongues.
I want you to make me reach for things
you swear to me aren't there.

I want you to flip me, hold me
with one arm around my waist,
press your stomach to my spine,
fall and rise with me,
slide into night with me.

And when morning offers the hush of sleep,
I want you to open your tired eyes,
wrap my hair around your fingers,
pull me closer and murmur: *Yes baby,
I promise I will be your toy.*

Where Her Flesh Begins

His hand brushed her breast as he reached
for the popcorn between her legs.

Scrummaging for puffed seeds he made
the cardboard container bang against her clit.

She moved the bucket to his crotch. As she reached
for the corn her arm brushed his erection; it was
old denim: soft, casual, sexual, hard.

Their drug-induced craving called them to switch
from salt to sugar. He made the miniature Snickers bar
melt in his mouth. He attacked her lips with his,
pushing the chocolate out of him and into her.

On the 15-block walk from Prospect Park
West to Grand Army Plaza they transformed
into two human beat boxes making rhythms
that slipped from their mouths to their hips.

At Grand Army, he sang, I love you
in a voice like Barry White.

She said, Sing it like Patti Labelle. And he did.
She said, Sing it like Mary J. Blige. And he did.
Sing it like Babyface. Say it like the President.
Say it, please say it, like Bill.

He said, Say I'm the man. She said,
I'm the man. He said, Say I'm the man
and grab your dick. She said, I'm the man,
and grabbed her dick. He said, Now grab mine.

On Eastern Parkway, she grabbed his dick
and his butt. He walked forwards as she walked
sideways. Her hands cupped around his denim
private parts like a diaper made of flesh.

The lights turned red. She let go.
They crossed. Cars held lines of faces
fascinated by the open-road peep show.

She led him over her threshold. He unsnapped
her bra. She pulled her breasts away from his face
until he drooled. He ate her until the mix of juice
and saliva formed a puddle on her couch.

She listened to his moans, deep and low.
She wanted to scream, Yes,
America, oral sex *is* sex.

He crashed into immediate sleep.
She lay still with him in her arms.
His weight made her limbs numb.

She drifted into the words of a holy union:
We have come here today to join together....

Hands still touching the small
of his back, she could not feel where
his flesh ended; where her flesh began.

The Space Between

Stuck in an unnamed place
half way between love and in love,
you call me late at night and ask
if I'm sleeping. I tell you, I'm writing.
You ask about what? Love, I say.

When I write about us, I stop myself
from saying *we make love* or *we have sex.*
I search for a euphemism that won't bind me,
won't define us. I arrive at the phrase
move together. And only now, in writing
this poem, do I see how fitting it is.

The way we moved together vertically
is what made me want to move with you
horizontally. Music joined us,
but even in this joining, I didn't know
how to behave, how much or how little
to say, how to choose to be me.

An old friend told me if I feel
smaller than myself with a lover
this is the wrong lover for me.

Yes, I make myself smaller; I shrink
my politics, my conversation. I shrink
in mind, but I grow in body.

And don't think I don't know
when the movements are fluid
we look for ways to draw each other
nearer, name each other soulmates.

I have been a two-time witness
to how easily the soul-thread can be
cut, leaving the so-called soulmate
dangling in an empty world of one.

The same old friend comes back
to say a lover should love
in me what I love in myself.

Trouble is, we don't know what we love
in each other. We exchange tapes of songs
to hint at the possibility of a feeling,
admitting nothing, partially exposed
in lyrics so, if pushed, we can deny
we meant the words that way.

We skirt around edges hoping
the space between will stop closeness
because close is where we are
fighting ourselves not to be.

I preach distance to you. I inflict it
on myself. I invent barriers like age-gaps
and bad-timing. But only now, in writing
this poem, do I learn how the word
distance can magnetize lovers.

You obey my demands. You don't
call. We don't speak. But you find
a strand of my hair in your freezer
and I still write with the taste of
you in my mouth.

Lessons In Honesty

(1)

We were two women sitting on a bed
and I said, If I could have one wish
I wish I could sing with a voice that made people cry.
And I felt what I said was a rare ruby.

And she said, I can't tell you what I wish
because just saying it makes me want to cry.

But I pushed her to say the words
and she said, I wish my sister could walk.

And in the silence, I felt selfish in her selflessness,
mean in her generosity, decadent in her sensitivity.

Wrapping her in my arms, we cried together
rocking as tears mixed with mucus.

And in this moment, I felt moved to kiss her
eyelids, nose, chin, and keep kissing her until
the soothing rocking changed rhythm
and moved into longing.

And in this moment, I felt what I always thought
was a masculine kind of hunger, but worst of all
the surfacing of a moment not shared
turning me into an unanchored buoy
drifting guiltily
out to sea.

(2)

We were two women sitting on a couch
and I said, I think there is no truth so bad
it can hurt as much as a lie.
And I meant what I said
right to my marrow.

And she said, I can't tell you what I think.
Just saying it will incriminate me.

But I pushed her to say the words. And she said,
Lying is the easiest thing in the world.

And in the silence, my body tightened with distrust,
shivered with unease, hardened for protection.

And in this moment, I wanted to take back
every truth I ever told her and wondered
how many of her truths had been lies.

And from that moment, I monitored her movements,
words, remembering the conversations of others
saying she's not to be trusted.

And from that moment, she said nothing
and did nothing suspect,
turning me into an unanchored buoy
drifting warily
out to sea.

(3)

We were two women sitting in a diner,
and she said, If you could have one wish
what would it be?

And I said, I can't tell you what I wish.
Just saying it makes me want to cry.

But she pushed me to say the words
so I wrote them on a napkin.

I wish I could make love for one night
with someone I loved and who was in love with me.

And in the silence, I felt vulnerable in my honesty,
needy in my revelation, tears in my eyes.

And in this moment
I watched words crumple in my fist,
using the napkin to wipe away
public tears I wanted to escape,
feeling angry at her for forcing me
into a truth I wanted to avoid.

And she, in a moment not shared,
turned me into an unanchored buoy
drifting defenseless
out to sea.

(4)

We were the same two women
sitting in the same diner
and I said, It's your turn.
What would you wish?
Be honest.

And she said, I was wondering
if we could ever have a relationship.

And in the silence,
I was shocked by her wish,
disappointed in her honesty,
cheated by the question.

And in this moment of discomfort
I suddenly understood the words
to that silly song by Nancy and Frank Sinatra:
And didn't I go and spoil it all
by saying something stupid.

And in this moment not shared
I turned her into an unanchored buoy
drifting embarrassed
out to sea.

Bang

You were an American in Amsterdam
exchanging your wedding ring
for 8 hours of balancing with me.
On a single mattress we connected
sex to god transforming
orgasms into answered prayers.

The next day we took a reprieve
to visit Anne Frank's house
too distracted by ourselves
to go beyond meditating on its smallness.

Continuing as reluctant tourists,
we took a boat ride where
an Ethiopian street-seller
made his hands into a gun, saying, *Bang!*
one of the few words of English
he knew to describe New York.

You flew back home hurt
the symbol of your city was a gun
in the minds of people who had
only visited through a TV screen.

You ran your fingers ragged
writing me 283 letters in a year
to convince me your home had
more to offer than guns.

Using the pile of blue air-mail
envelopes as evidence of love,
I flew to New York to be won.

The first day of my new job
you sat outside for 3¹/₂ hours
because you didn't know
what time I'd finish and
you just wanted to be there.

It took a month before
you removed your lenses,
allowing me to see you in glasses,
one of the few signs of weakness
shooting past the surface of your skin.

Staring now, at the dent in the wall
I see you hurling plates
and me ducking, watching the gash
you planned for my body
slice my desk instead.

My desk—the only part of the apartment
that belonged to me. I was squeezed
into the wooden corner of a bedroom
where our balancing act now belonged
to a silent circus that had long moved out.

I looked for connections between
the you that was and the you who
changed your name and became the hand
coming for me, snatching my vest,
pulling me away from the window.

It wasn't till the next day
when I saw red marks on my body
I understood why I felt beaten.

You took away my knife and fork.
Eat with your hands, you said.
It's Kwanzaa and this is how
they eat in Africa.

Afraid to ask which country you chose
to represent the continent this evening,
I remembered eating pureed Ethiopian food
and attempted to roll a pork chop
into a mound I could throw
in my mouth with my fingers.

The food dropped and I dared to say,
A chop is not appropriate for rolling.
I rose to get a fork and you said,
Pick up that fork and I'll take away your keys.

You took my keys and I took my passport to work,
thinking it was the only thing I needed
to escape the whisper I'd become—
a person so stunned I didn't know how
to suck out the bullet that was you.

Go

The newspapers reported that Elvis was found
dead, on his bathroom floor, with his pants curled
around his ankles. A doctor analyzed his bowel
movements for the cause of death—straining
had made his blood pressure rise, and he dropped
like the tear falling into the food of a woman
sitting in a restaurant when a thin woman
two tables away points at her and says,
People that fat can't wipe when they go.
It's true, I saw it on Oprah.

I Will Not Grow Old Wishing

112 pounds make me the heaviest woman
in my dance class—pounds distributed
in places making it impossible to deny
I have the body of a nourished woman.

Full breasts and rounded hips.
My ballet teacher calls me Sophia Loren
as his eyes fix on my breasts.
He dares them to move as I jump
sixty-four times in first position.

Wanting the attention to go away
from my breasts, I concentrate
on making the body parts disappear
by living on fruit for days.

By the end of the week, I buy
four chocolate cupcakes. I push
them into my mouth one after the other.
I stand in the street to eat. I can't wait
the fifty yard walk to my door.

At the supermarket, my 98 pound friend selects
ice cream, apple pie, fried chicken—
my insides frappé in disgust.

She leaves my house not having touched
the ice cream and pie. I finish the chicken
as soon as the front door slams behind her.

I eat ice cream and pie as a midnight snack,
breakfast, lunch, and dinner and then
make a plan to give me back to myself.

I'm tired of being told
I'm all wrong to plié,
pirouette, fouetté—
whip into shape.

Food protects me
from a jump,
a teacher, a man,
a woman, sex.

In my twenties, I fall in love.
I don't eat or sleep for two weeks.
I sit up all night, breathing
to the sound of a saxophone
until I become so thin
friends tell me to go
to a doctor who tells me
I'm sick with love.

The first time my lover takes me home
his mother walks about the house
with cooking chocolate in her apron.
She wants to stop him from hiding
in the bathroom to eat it before dinner.

He waltzes over to the mayonnaise
tablespooning his need to be something
straight into his mouth.

Settling into our nest
I cook our first meal.

I'm happy, he's asking for
a second helping.

In my smile he sees a sneer.

I tell him, No, I do not think you're greedy.
I tell him, No, I don't know what projecting means.
No, I've never met anyone who goes to therapy.
No, I don't think I'm living with a fruitcake.
I don't know why I chose the word fruitcake.
I'm not making fun of you.
I tell him, No. I stop eating for days.

I call Maria. She says, You've got to eat something.

I make a turkey sandwich, pour a Diet Coke.
The sandwich triggers something.
I eat potato salad then walk to digest my food.

Passing Baskin Robbins I buy
a double scoop of mocha and pistachio
on a sugar cone. Back home,
I eat a small box of Cheezits
with two glasses of milk.

I can't stop I'm so hungry.

I go back out, buy a pint of chocolate ice cream,
eat it all, then make a peanut butter sandwich.
By this time it's midnight, and I feel guilty.

I try to feel better by eating healthy things:
carrots, celery, radishes, sweet gherkins,
pickled vegetables, spiced cauliflower.

I'm depressed, but I'm not disgusted.

I eat and eat until my eyes are gone
disappearing into my face—bloated,
floating in a river of leftovers.

I take a photo album to work.
The supervisor says, You looked
beautiful at your sister's wedding.
You must have been 30 pounds lighter.

She's the supervisor—the one who gets higher
pay for knowing more than me—doesn't she know
a bigger body means I have more places to bruise?

I tell the supervisor,
my teachers, my lovers,
want me like this or leave me.

My lover leaves.
I start a slow suicide
going for twelve hour days
with only one French fry,
hip-bones sticking out from a leotard,
sacrificing food for someone to love me.

My body shrinks two sizes
and I give myself
a double scoop of loathing:
hate for my body as it was,
hate for my body as it is.

I see people struggle,
should they say
the loss looks good?

At work, the man
who empties my garbage
asks me if I'm sick
and I feel loved.

I see myself struggle.
Should I wear looser, tighter clothing?

I know it's impossible
to look androgynous in a T-shirt
if my breasts need a C cup.

The need to be attractive and
the need to be true to myself
continue to spar inside me.

Struggling against last bites—
morsels that will leave me full—
I walk around hungry, but
I don't want to die this way.

Will I grow old wishing
I am someone else's body?

Will I grow old wishing
I am somebody else?

Questions In The Mind Of A Poet
While She Washes Her Floors

Will obedience leave me unknown to myself, stranded?

Is it enough for me to know where I'm from?

If I do more truth-telling will I be happier with what I say?

If I had three days to live would I still be sensible?

Is the break between my feelings and my memory
the reason I'm unable to sustain rage?

Am I a peninsula slowly turning into an island?

If I grew up gazing at the ocean would I think
life came in waves?

If I were a nomad would I measure time
by the length of a footstep?

If I can see a cup drop to the floor and shatter
why can't I see it gather itself back together?

If a surgeon cut out my mistakes
would the scar be under my heart?

How much time will I spend protecting myself
from what the people I love call love?

Would my desires feel different if I lived forever?

Will my desires destroy my politics?

Is taboo sex the ultimate aphrodisiac?

If I fall in love with the wrong person
how do I learn to un–in love myself?

Can I make my intuition into a divining rod?

Is music the closest I can get to God?

How many of these questions will remain
when I kneel to wash my floors again?

If I Could Touch Faith
This Poem Would Not Exist

If it is true that to write about something I have to touch it—

not a metaphorical touch, but actual fingers outstretched,

palms flat against whatever my imagination demands

I take for my next question—then perhaps this is why

I have never written about faith. I know my hands will

never know the feel of faith's flesh; my fingers will never

be spread across faith's body; my palms will never know

the curve of faith's form. The only touch of faith I can feel

is the palm of one hand flat against the palm of the other,

in prayer, in the hope that faith will come to me as a poem.

Divination

I think I found God today
while pouring olive oil
into a glass of cold water
watching the shapes move like
green seahorses to tell
the story of my future.

I think I found God today
while peeling a pomegranate
into a yellow china bowl
watching the seeds bleed red
over my fingers to tell
the story of my future.

I think I found God today
while kissing a heart
in a black blanket sky
floating between planets
Saturn and Jupiter to tell
the story of my future.

I think I found God today
while cutting my hair
into a white porcelain sink
watching the strands form
a constellation of stars to tell
the story of my future.

I think I found God today
while watching men bathe
in a blue and white fountain;
in water they became women
with thick hair and full lips to tell
the story of my future.

I think I found God today
while I slept under an olive tree
having sacred dreams of snowdrops
growing out of tears and trees
on their knees telling
the story of my future.

Sinkyone Woman Living

*The Sinkyone are people indigenous to a part of the northern
California coast called the Sinkyone Wilderness. From 1850 to 1870
the U.S. military and settlers came to the area massacring most of
this community. Sally Bell was a name given to a young native
woman who witnessed and survived the murder of her family.*

If I had found you hiding in the brush
the lone survivor when the stone-hearted came

to kill your kin, take away your wilderness,
I would not have called you sally bell.

I would have asked your name and if
I didn't catch it I would have listened to you

repeat the sound until the word fell off my tongue.
I would not have taken you in but helped you

build a home, your own place to rest.
And once finished, I would have taken

my blue sheet, sprinkled it with watery oil
made from eucalyptus leaves and spread

the ocean-colored square outside your doorway.
I would have waited until the morning fog cleared

and the grieving Pacific joined the melancholy sky,
until you finished sweeping, until you came to greet me.

I would have asked you to sit, poured oil
over your feet, used my fingers to soothe

the pacific waves of your wrinkling skin.
I would have made your toenails shine

like baby abalone shells collecting on the beach.
I would have stopped to hear your breath as

the stroke of my hand released you into a stillness
that has been hard to feel since you knelt among

the lifeless bodies and flying spirits of your people
clutching the still warm heart of your younger sister—

a carved out muscle faintly pumping
the last beat of love with an ancestral echo

only to be heard by a living Sinkyone
woman, only to be heard by one.

Zen And The Art Of Flower Arranging

You give me lavender roses at breakfast and orange roses at dinner. I pull off the petals and put them in Saran Wrap. I want them to stay soft while you're away. I imagine unwrapping them to make a rose-petal blanket for our bed. But then Buddha comes to me and asks, *Who do you think you are to dismember flowers in the name of love?* My guilt blooms. The Brooklyn Botanic Garden and the grounds of Windsor Castle combined cannot hold its size. I want to ask for Buddha's forgiveness, but I don't want to waste The Enlightened One's time. Instead, I pace The Garden, apologizing to the roses, waiting for you to arrange the golden-skinned calla lily in my bed.

Floating Poem

I was a virgin walking through the Virgin
Megastore for the first time. With you,
even browsing in a CD supermarket is an event—
a pristine moment. When 18 video monitors
make 18 Janet Jacksons appear, you demand,
Look. And I do. And the image makes me want
to rush home to write a poem. But when
I put fingers to keyboard, I can't decide
what inspires me more—the 18 Janet Jacksons
floating naked in water or our two heads pressed
together as I share a set of headphones with you.

Remembrance Of Things Past

I wake up, turn on my computer, then go pee.
I make decaf coffee with powdered milk. I take
one multivitamin, one vitamin C, two calciums
with added vitamin D. I don't want my body to crumble.
Next stop, the bathroom to splash water on my face.
I squeeze cleanser on cotton to remove the stubborn
traces of mascara under my eyes. I go back to the corner
of my bedroom that is my study. I sit at the computer.
I stand up again. I make the bed. I sit. I stand. I go
into the living room, turn on the TV. I check the weather.
It's cold and cloudy. I wonder why I left England.
The TV says there is a Battle Against Breast Cancer.
I go back to my made bed and lie down. I check my breasts.
It's been two years since my last exam. I hold my breath.
I press circles around my nipples. No lumps. I exhale.
I call myself a silly cow. I stand up and flatten the lumps
I've made in the quilt. I go back to the computer.
I click on the icons. The computer says, *You've got mail.*
The voice does not sound like a friend or a superstar.
Why can't Bette Midler give me my daily mail?
And why are all the e-mails I get virus alerts?
I want to click on an e-mail from Madonna. I want her
to invite me to a millennium party. I want us to
take off our bras and paint our breasts with henna.
Bette Midler says: *Honey, Do You Have Mail!*

Madonna@hotmail writes: *I'm not going out New Year's Eve.*
Elena@chickmail writes: *But it's the end of the millennium.*
Get a sitter. Madonna writes: *I'd rather spend time at home*
with Lola. Elena writes: *Sigh. OK. Let me know if you change*
your mind. The climax to the end of the century is going to be
an anticlimax. I log off and go into Microsoft Word. I like that
it's called Word. Word is a good word. I click on the draft
of last night's poem. It's called *Unvalentine.* This is a bad title.
It is a bad poem. But! It has some nice lines. I'm on the eighth
draft, trying to salvage it. The poem wants to go in a direction
different from the one I planned. I want a phone conversation
between ex-lovers, on Valentine's Day, to explore how two people
remember the same past. But the poem wants nothing to do
with Valentine's Day. It wants to find meaning
in the smell of Egypt, the taste of figs and, of course,
the perennial, love. The poem and I are playing tug-of-war.
I'm losing. I walk to the refrigerator and pour a protein shake.
If I play my cards right—march confidently into the new
millennium, keep up with the tofu and calcium, then
the onset of menopause should be a minor hiccup.
I daydream out the living room window. I'm searching
for the place where the poem and I meet. What if
I work from a new direction? Change its name.
Call it *Remembrance of Things Past.*
But it's been a long century and I bet
someone has already used that title.

Approaching The Third Millennium
(found poem)

Jerusalem Forecasts Sudden Surge Of 'Saviors'
New York Times 11/26/99

Jerusalem's main psychiatric clinic expects
a surge in admissions in the year 2000—
the beginning of Christianity's third millennium.

If predictions are true, cases will increase 100 percent.
The clinic has built a new emergency room.

Doctors are treating foreigners—Jews,
Christians, and Muslims overwhelmed by
the religious magnetism of the sacred city.

The disorder, most common among pilgrims from the U.S.
and Europe, is called *Jerusalem Syndrome.*

The afflicted are convinced they are biblical figures:
King David, John the Baptist, the Virgin Mary, and Jesus.

Ages range from 17 to 70. The average is 35
with above average levels of education.

Some come with visions of the end of the world,
others don white robes—sheets from their hotel beds—

and take to the streets to preach Jesus-like sermons.
Israel has already expelled 60 Christian cultists with

apocalyptic fantasies of un-godly millennial mayhem.

Intimate Mixture

I have electricity in me.
If lightning strikes me, I can die.
If I don't pick up my feet as
I cross a carpet, I make sparks fly.

I think about this as my electricity starts
to jump over the synapses of my dendrites.
And my body goes *bam!* and I say, Good God!
Lightning strike me dead, right here.
Now I've seen you,
there's nothing more to live for.

But lightning doesn't strike.
And I remain standing as my endorphins
kick it to my adrenal hormones.
And my parasympathetic system
overpowers my sympathetic system.
And my heart starts speeding,
and my blood increases flow to muscles
I use for big time physical attraction,
and instead of dropping dead and dying
I look at you and say, Hello.

We dance. We talk. We dance some more.
I take you home. I hand you the record.
You wipe away the dust. And as your arm
makes circles on vinyl, our attraction builds.
Smokey sings. Our clothes stick together.

You touch me. I smell the mist
around your neck. You take off your shirt

with one hand, pull me closer with the other.
We're opposite. We attract. We undress.

With oil, I sweeten your wrist, you perfume
my breasts. You put your mouth to my hipbone,
I burst into the flashing light of a firefly.
I put my mouth to your thigh, you grow wings
that spread into the song of a hummingbird.

We kiss until our lip-prints are so familiar
we could track each other down next time
either one of us commits a love crime.

We rock until we make heart-shaped sweat.
We burn candles. We burn fuses.
There is so much fire between us I hear NASA
counting down 5 4 3 2 1. And damn,
I swear, we definitely have lift-off.

Woman And Machine

Last time you called I told you not to.
I said I needed space. *Space.* I never use

that word. I hung up feeling like a relic
from the seventies. You waited three days

before you called again. You said you felt
like an addict trying to go cold turkey. You

said you felt like running away and towards
at the same time. Instead, you dialed my number

while fantasies distracted you with our first kiss
under the burst of your shower and daydreams

took you to new purple sheets and fresh love.
By the time you came back to solid life

the operator's voice cued you to:
Hang up and try your call again.

I erased recognition from my voice;
to not give you a clue I knew

exactly what you meant; that
I'd imagined my phone ringing

when the music was loud enough
to mask its sound; that I'd run

from bedroom to living room, chasing
phantom doorbells; paused the CD player;

scanned the red light on my answer machine
to see if it flashed; checked my e-mail,

voice-mail, and any audio device I could lay
my ears on to see if you'd called. When you left

a message saying: *I miss you so much,*
I knew you'd spread the feeling on extra thick,

but I still pushed 8 on my voice-mail
to save you; to play you back when

I need a voice to inject in my ear— a 911 hit
of sugar, smooth and sweet to ease my need for

molasses; brown, thick, and slow like
the sound of you singing my name.

The Science Of Kissing

My brain holds neurons that help me locate

small parts of your body when the lights go out.

These neurons act as sensors and are activated

by my body's movement, others are activated

by your touch. For example, when a part of my body—

let's say my lips—is placed near an area of your body—

let's say your lips—the neurons responsible for

our baby flowers of flesh turn on. So when

I want to kiss you in the dark, my mouth will

always find your mouth—the neurons will remember

where your mouth is located. My sensor cells will

guide me until I feel the taste of your tongue.

If Picasso Had Loved Women

We smoke the joint shotgun. You rush your lips against mine—
your design to touch me without naming it a kiss.

I watch the blue smoke curl about your face—
framing you into a painting Picasso might have created

had he loved women. I draw toward you with the smoke,
charting the rise of your breasts under my tongue,

mapping the sweep of your hips with my nose.
I romp in the geometry of your body.

The canvas blazes. You ask for water.
I run ice along the length of your forehead.

It drips. I watch. You lick your top lip
and I grow jealous ice can melt.

From Where I Stand

Monet tires of painting lilies.

He drops before me to paint
a pubic prayer—a V of tender
black strokes.

He holds his palette
in one hand, brushes in the other,
the smaller ones clenched between his teeth.

From where I stand I notice
the top of his head, his hair is thinning.

I snatch a brush from his mouth
to color his crown. I paint in his hair
with long strokes as he paints in mine.

We are the gods of hair.
We let this power go to our heads.

We paint short strands in unexpected places—
on all sides of the Eiffel Tower.

We turn this landmark into a bearded rod,
erect, reaching to disturb a cloud.

                    But wait.

What makes hair special is how it comes
in small ways, in small places:

the pit under our arms, the arcs over our eyes,
the expanse across our shins, the circles that cover our heads,
the half moons that recede and eventually abandon.

I feel another artist inside me.
                              Yes,
I feel his brush strokes swirling.

He is painting the walls of my womb
with stars and a turbulent sky.

He is singing: *To make blue you need yellow and orange.*
Monet recognizes this voice. He tells me
van Gogh has crawled in my uterus to paint.

Van Gogh dives into delirium.

He paints an olive tree on my ribcage.
I lean on the tree while he slaps on more blue.
The wildness of his strokes knocks me off balance.

I lie on my bed. His painting swells my stomach.
Van Gogh's head presses against my cervix.

I feel myself widen. My contractions produce sky.
My labor pains make stars. After a day of pushing,
I give birth to a *Starry Night*.

I look down at the canvas of my skin.
Monet has finished. He has painted
thirteen silver crescent moons hiding
in the curls of my triangular night sky.

I part his thinning strands to kiss his head.
He stands and kisses each of my cheeks.

As the tip of his mustache brushes my lip,
I think of my own hair and how
it brushes my own lips, how it curves
to hold my folds in its crook. It's gentle—

a dainty army that shuffles towards
this cloister between my legs.
The hairs cry into this sanctum: *Create*.

Monet is captivated.

Sugar And Pepper

(1)

As you stoop over homework at the dining table
your mother makes curried chicken at the stove.
The smell of almost-ready wafts under your nose,
Come here. Taste this. What does it need?
A bit more pepper, you say. She nods, pinches
the black grain between her fingers and takes
a journey around the pot, sprinkling with one hand,
stirring with the other. *How's this now?* she asks,
holding the wooden spoon up to your mouth,
her hand cupped under your chin so the curried
liquid will not spill on her freshly polished floors.
It needs more chili. More curry, maybe?
She takes a taste, raises one eyebrow and says,
Hmm, hmm, you like it hot. A week later she calls
from work and asks you to take the chicken out
to defrost. The following week, she calls
to ask you to chop the onions. A month later,
she calls to ask you to start frying the chicken
with sugar to make it brown. And after six months
of asking you to chop, fry, and stir she calls and says,
Baby, I have to work late. Will you cook the curry
for me? You hesitate. Eventually, you say, *Yes*
Mama, and then you retrace the time she's spent
preparing you for the day she asks you to cook and
you cannot say, *But Mama, I don't know how.*

(2)

As I stoop over my homework at the dining table
the smell of you wafts into my mind. I fantasize
about the day you will take me for a drive, a kiss,
a journey that will leave me spinning into your kitchen.
You will ask me to, *Come here.* You will ask me to,
Taste this. You will ask me if the food needs more pepper.
I will nod. You will tell me to taste it again, then kiss me
and make the curried liquid flow between our mouths.
And it will burn. And you will raise one eyebrow and say,
Hmm, hmm. You like it hot. A week later, you will call
from work and ask me to take the chicken out to defrost.
The following week you will ask me to chop the onions.
A month later, you will ask me to start frying, you will
remind me to add the sugar to make it brown. And after
six months of asking me to chop, fry, and stir, you will
call me and say, *Baby, I have to work late. Will you cook
the curry for me?* I will hesitate. Eventually, I will say
yes, and I will try not to notice you are preparing me for
the day you will call to say you are never coming home.

Hymn

Beauty is the lover's path to the spirit—only the path, only a means.
                                          Thomas Mann, *Death In Venice*

Beauty rides the #5 train. Two tiger's eyes roar
quietly out from his chestnut face. A thin layer of
white dust covers his boots, jeans, skin. This earthly
representation of heaven is a construction worker.

He folds his arms. His black T-shirt has POLO
written across the front. It rides up an inch
to expose a tattoo on each bicep—a flaming sun
on one, a partially hidden swirl on the other.

I spy a tiny diamond above the curve
of one delicate nostril. I take Beauty
to Tiffany's. I buy him an engagement ring
I buy him breakfast. I love him.

He exposes the second tattoo. I see the letters *CA.*
Are those his initials? Is that his lover's name,
or an ex-lover, or a one night stand—alcohol,
a kiss, an image indelibly penned into his skin,
a reminder of a moment he has lived to regret?

But what am I saying? He has no regrets.
If he has ever made a mistake, he does not
know it or he has not been held accountable.
He is too beautiful to be held accountable.

He chews gum. I watch his mouth move.
I see his jaw, his lips in action. I am the gum

in his mouth. His teeth push into my flesh.
His tongue covers me. His saliva is my River
Ganges. His mouth makes me holy.

His wrists are stiff. He makes circles with his hands.
His hands circle me. He lays them on my body.
His touch brings me back to life; makes me walk,
talk. I thank him for the miracle.

His T-shirt reads APOLLO. God lives among us.
He rises. I rise. The train arrives at Nevins Street.
We change from the #5 to the #3. It is our church.
It takes me deeper into Brooklyn, towards home.
I ride beside him and I am closer, my God, to thee.

Close Communion

Did you notice the closest I have come to touching you
is your thigh pressed against mine as the train rocks us

closer on our rides from work to our separate homes?
If you closed your eyes would you recognize my scent

on the platform? Would you follow the trail of my aroma
to sit by me? When I get up to go, does your heart burst

into an orchestra of Kyoto drummers
pounding: *Don't leave. Don't leave?*

Can I shape you into a fantasy who walks me to my door?
Will I pluck up the nerve to bring the illusion of you inside,

introduce you to my furniture, the flowers on my wall,
my CDs? Do you know that since our thighs first met

I have been in close communion with Ella Fitzgerald?
She sings me a hymn: *Every time we say goodbye I die*

a little. I have counted 100 daydreams where I am trying
to rescue the refrain of this song from becoming a dirge.

Can I tell you about daydream 101? I hide my pot
for one, pull out the teapot for two. We join in sips

of jasmine tea—our libation. The baptized petals float
to the surface. As you raise my china cup to your mouth

the tea glues a petal to your top lip.
This vision drives me to daydream

102—you, feasting on a flower.

Miracle

I went to see the pyramids and stood beside a blind man.
He said, Tell me what you see. I said, 500 feet of rock
reaching to the sun.

I took him to the pyramid base and said, Touch.
But hand on stone was not enough.
Do you want to know how high they reach?
I'll show you. Come.

My name is Saha, I said. Can you say Sa ha?
Like Sahara but I am not a desert. I see
more than a few days of rain a year and
my footsteps are as liquid as a camel's.

I flowed forward and he sailed with me to market.
We stood by the mango seller and I made the blind man
smell all 36 types of mangoes Cairo had to offer.

I bought one of each. We went to his hotel room.
I made a circle with the 35 mangoes around his bed.
The 36th mango I held under his nose.

He inhaled and flooded into me like Egypt's black gold—oil.
He set us on fire. While the flames baptized our bodies,
he knelt on the floor feeling for the largest mango he could find.

He guided the fruit to my nose. I inhaled and softened into him
like Egypt's white gold—cotton. I wrapped him in 500 feet of
reaching to the sun—I gave him light.

Holy Rumor

Someone, I can't mention names, said
Jesus is in love with a band of Australian Aborigines

who have limited the time they spend working.
They devote four hours to labor.

The rest of the day they dedicate to art.
The Aborigines sit in the sun painting each other's bodies

with words like *hallelujah* and *honeysuckle*
while Jesus stoops to kiss the back of their necks

and the tips of their fingers. Rumor has it,
Jesus feeds off the men's stamens and the women's pistils.

This person told me that Jesus is also in love with the sea.
She rose early and caught him lying naked at the water's edge.

She hid behind a hedge for an hour and saw
the waves lap and lick his body. She swears she heard

Jesus whispering, *Oh my God,*
my God. She saw him

roll to his knees, put his mouth to the waves and blow until
the current flowed and swelled and crashed.

Sadly Mistaken

I have not learned how sleep comes to you
in seconds; how you wake to fierce morning
showers and iron your clothes naked to MTV.

I have not learned that you lotion your body
with almond oil. And I certainly have not
learned how that lotion makes your ring slip

off your hand and fit easily on the index finger
of mine. Also, it's not true that your skin makes me
wonder if velvet is edible. And it is also not true

I have learned the weight of your thigh as it rests
on my thigh as we are sleeping. No, I have never
wanted to trace the outline of the wild cat tattooed

on your calf. And I have never ever wanted that cat
to climb off your leg and hand me the lily in its mouth.
No, I have not spent all year fantasizing about making

your lips my home. And if you should ever think
I have learned cloves are the secret spice you drop
in a pot of rice you would be sadly mistaken. And

if you think you are the first person I call to look
at the moon when it's full, you are simply wrong.
Well yes, perhaps I have grown a little accustomed

to the ballads you sing me down the telephone.
But if anyone ever told you these songs have
made me cry, well, of course, they were lying.

The State Of Our Union *(Redemption Song)*

Alone in our homes, connected by the phone,
I inhale from my joint as you roll yours.
You tell me to mute the TV.

Our thumbs rule the kingdom of the remote.
In sync, we press. We rob the President of his voice
as he addresses the State of the Union.

You replace the President's overture with a voiceover
of what you imagine is his internal dialogue and
you repeat this with every politician delivered
across our prime-time screens.

The grass returns us to adolescence. We giggle
at your descriptive mix of presidential body parts
grinding into female cabinet members
converting bureaucrats into players
involved in a high-level game of Twister.

As the President fades into a sea of suits,
you tell me to turn off my lights, watch
the screen and listen to the music
coming from your CD player to my ear.

The TV images blur as Marley sings, *Old Pirates,*
Yes they rob I. The purity of his voice wipes out
the sound of Eastern Parkway and we are
suspended in a four minute forever.

And in this four minutes Redemption Song
releases my own imaginings. And I wonder

what you would have as my internal dialogue
if we were to mute the sound of my voice.

Would you know that two mornings a week
I wonder if I'm in love with you? That on this
duet of days my thoughts begin with my own
combination of our body parts entwined,
rising to sing songs of freedom, in unity.

Would you know that my morning meditations play
themselves out with you ironing my clothes
while I make us Kool-Aid and mint tea for breakfast?

And would you know that after every one of these
daybreak fantasies I promise myself I will not
learn to love you, that like a politician,
my tactics add up to hiding myself
with smiles that never show what I think?

A Sexual Revolution:
From Punk Rock To Soul

I was 16 in 1977
when the young British working class
opened their legs wide
under the guidance of Malcolm McClaren
and gave birth to Punk Rock
giving me the excuse to disrobe
from a flower power purple theory of peace
and re/dress myself in the bright red
political theories of a revolution
I didn't fully understand
except I knew my socialist tendencies
and being able to quote The Clash lyrics
would get me a smile
and a proverbial pat on my back
from the other 16-year-old pothead, wannabe radicals
disguised by the ripped jeans, guitars and U.B. 40s
they wore like badges of working class honor
and when we sang

beat the drum tonight, alfonso
spread the news all over the world
the big meeting has decided on total war

instead of wondering where I was gonna find a machete
and how was I gonna run with the dog pack to survive
I was still back on the first line
wondering who the hell Alfonso was
because I hadn't seen any sugar fields
or cotton plantations in London
and I'd never seen the Sandinistas

wandering around the flowery suburb we lived in
but I knew if The Clash was singing about this man
I could relax long enough for the music to push me forward
until we both lost our voices from shouting their songs over
the engine of your tin can roaring down the highway like
the inflated ego of a Renault 5 that thinks it's a brand new BMW
on our way back from our middle class trip to France
where I'd let you go further than your fingers
discovering full fledged sex for the first time
we didn't leave our hotel room for the whole 2 weeks
making a holiday out of sexual positions blended together
with the French cream cheese you spread
over my no longer private parts and since that day
cream cheese has never looked the same to me
and Sinead sings

it's been 7 hours and [2,920] days
since you took your love away

but that's alright
our love wasn't really passion
but brother and sisterly
we even had the same last name,
skin color, hair texture, culture and class
but you changed from a 4-year-old
who watched bread turning
into toast for entertainment
into a 23-year-old with full
membership to the British Film Theatre
and I changed from a 4-year-old
who preferred books to dolls
into a 23-year-old who wanted someone
to get nasty with on dance floors
so you traded me in for a couple of our friends
on your way to a new girlfriend

and I traded in Punk Rock for Soul
but I—a former teenage revolutionary—
knew George Michael was really a Smokey Robinson rip-off
and the radicals we knew would never have given him
the award as the best R&B male vocalist
and we were quick to turn up our noses
at those politically ignorant Americans
who managed to give birth to The Black Panthers
but still didn't know who Tommy Smith was
and even though we were only 7
at the time of the '68 Olympic Games we grew into teenagers
with pictures of Tommy Smith taped to our bedroom walls
clutching his gold medal in one hand
and holding his black power fist high with the other
but it was much safer to play George Michael
than Smokey Robinson in '82
as the sound of Smokey was dangerously close
to that flower power shit we were trying to run away from
and I bet you were glad when George Michael became famous
because people stopped telling you
you look like Tony Curtis
and besides,
you, George Michael, and me
all had the same last name
you, George Michael, and me
three Cypriots from Finchley—
Cypriots from Finchley
how much more ordinary can you get?
George Michael escaped the ordinary by becoming famous
and I escaped by coming to America where

god save [steve mc] queen
and this [capitalist] regime

is the '90s version of The Sex Pistols' lyrics

and I hold onto my socialism for dear life
because it's so much easier to be corrupted
when you've lost your virginity
and talking about pistols and virgins
I was 23 before I made love by candlelight
and literally knocking into the flame
I made the sheets catch fire
and I still have the scorch mark on my duvet to prove it
and I was 25 before I took my first bubble bath
with a lover and Teddy Pendergrass singing

let's take a shower
a shower together

another lover making day and night merge
making me lie down on a larger-than-queen-size bed
naked with the floor looking like the inside of
an expensive lingerie store at the end of a one day sale
making my body slide underneath your thighs
my back arch in your palms turning me
on my stomach while you kneel by my side
tracing the length of my spine with your tongue
while slipping your hand between my legs
hoping I will ask you for more
but instead I remember Sinead again
and realize I can never make love
to a revolutionary song saying

england's not the mythical land
of madam george and roses
it's the home of police who kill
black boys on mopeds

and the only revolution I ever got close to was sexual
and here I am singing with a new lover

a lover who loves my love
but because of history
hates herself for loving me
because I don't know if I could
kill my grandmother if she was a racist
because I don't know if I could pack a gun
in the name of a war against white people
because sometimes I want to make love
instead of talking about The Revolution
and because sometimes I want to make love
instead of talking about The Revolution
I had to end the relationship
with my new lover
but not before we sang

if this world were mine

and even though we made love
to the velvet voice of Luther
I knew the song belonged to the '60s
and I shake my head at myself as I realize
making love and love songs go together so well—
they're fortunate to share the same soul,
to have and to hold, from this day forward
as long as they both shall live—Soul

The Motown Angel

Yesterday, I went to the supermarket. To get the maximum amount of pleasure from putting what I want in my cart, and going home with it, I stood in the produce section and imagined I could hear singing coming from the aisle which housed the jellies, fruit spreads, etc.

My C-Town usually blasts RuPaul spinning bass-thumping club music, but the singing I could hear sounded like a Motown angel who'd dropped from heaven.

As I moved down aisle three, standing there, singing, dipping his finger into a jar of orange-blossom honey was the Motown Angel himself, Mr. Marvin Gaye.

When he saw me, instead of trying to hide what he was doing, he asked if I wanted to share the jar of honey with him. Now, imagine, if Marvin Gaye asked you to share a jar of honey, what would you say? I said, Okay Marvin, but on one condition, that you take me home and sing, *Mercy, Mercy, Me.* He agreed.

I didn't care that the cashier looked at me as though I'd lost my mind for not being able to wait until I got home to dip my finger in the honey. I knew she couldn't see Marvin, being that he was a ghost and all. I imagined she thought I was high on grass and my behavior due to an extreme case of the munchies.

When we got home, I thought Marvin and I might have sex after that little finger-licking honey episode, but I think he could feel I had a lot on my mind, so he suggested we talk instead.

I offered him some fruit though, and he chose a pomegranate. I think he did this on purpose; it was definitely the one piece of fruit in my fruitbowl which took the longest to peel and separate, and I had a strong impression he wanted to stretch out the time we could spend together.

He separated every single red seed, made a mountain out of the bite-sized blood crystals and put them in a clear glass bowl. He took a teaspoon and fed me scoops of pomegranate seeds while we talked about love.

Marvin, I said, what would you do if you'd noticed you and your lover had replaced love-making on a Sunday morning, with holding hands while reading the paper; that you'd replaced skipping meals to make love, with going shopping for food; that you'd replaced not waiting to shower before making love, with choosing to watch TV even though your bodies are clean enough to be traveled with tongues?

He didn't answer immediately. Even ghosts have to think, I thought. But when he did open his mouth, instead of talking he sang, *Mercy, mercy, me—things ain't what they used to be.*

Marvin, I said. I want to make love so badly. I say it like a mantra, like a poem about a lover leaving, a poem about loss.

I want to kiss. And I know a kiss is more than a kiss; I know it can come straight at you, or tease you, or speak to you and say I want you, but not just yet, I want you to wait until your wanting spills over my thigh.

I want a lover to hold at a distance, examine like a child looking at a slice of watermelon wondering how she'll fit the whole piece in her mouth. I even want to act like a teenager standing on the train with my body pressed against my lover, kissing.

Sometimes, Marvin, I fantasize about being my lover's wisdom teeth, held captive in the back of her mouth, only able to see daylight when someone says something to make her laugh from her belly; a laugh big enough for her lips to fly open and show me a glimpse of the outside world. I have to find a way to dig all this up, resurrect it, but I'm not sure how.

I know how, said Marvin. Take off your clothes and kneel by your CD player and pray. I felt self-conscious taking off all my clothes in front of Marvin Gaye, but I did it anyway. I knelt and I prayed.

Get up, God said, and put on Marvin's music.

As the words to Sexual Healing began to fill my living room I noticed a young dancer standing where Marvin had been, moving like the only reason God had given her a body was to dance.

I watched her dance. She fell in love. I remembered that the last time I fell in love was also the last time I felt beautiful.

The young dancer traced the outline of the scar on my stomach with her tongue and told me how lucky I was to be able to wear my history like a map across my body. Her words made me realize how little love I've been prepared to accept for fear of not getting any at all.

The dancer said goodbye to me three times. I think she did this on purpose because it gave her three opportunities to run her five fingers along my back. On the third touch the dancer faded and Marvin came back.

Marvin, I said. Why is the person I want to touch, the one I can't put my arms around? Why is the one I want to look at, the one who takes away my capacity for direct eye contact? And why is the one I want to walk down the street with, the one who makes me run in the opposite direction? Makes me forget how to construct sentences; forget brand names of chocolates, so I stand there, feeling like a fool, as the words Bar of Mars tumble out of my mouth, and the only thing I can think to do is make a casual face and pretend I meant to say Mars Bar like that.

But this is my big question, Marvin. Why is the lover I want to stay home with, the one who leaves?

I don't know the answer to your question, Marvin said, but what I've learned is this. Do you remember how sweet the taste of our hello was?

Yes, I responded.

Well, in the same way you dipped your finger in the honey, right there, in the supermarket and didn't wait to go home to do it, that's the way to approach love.

I'm going to change back into the young dancer, now, and I want you to dip your finger in her. I want you to tell her that you need her to dance with you and I promise, if you tell her what you need she will try her best to keep dancing to the taste of your words.

But, Marvin, will her best be enough?

It will be, if she chooses music that moves you, if she dances as though you share a body; and if she leaves you dancing after the music has stopped.

Photo: Lisa Ross

Elena Georgiou is the recipient of a New York Foundation for the Arts poetry fellowship and the Astraea Foundation Emerging Writers Award in poetry. Her work has been published in numerous literary journals and anthologies. She teaches poetry and creative writing at Hunter College and City College of the City University of New York. She lives in Brooklyn.